DISNEY · PIXAR

a bug's life

Special Collector's Edition

A Behind-the-Scenes Look at How a Computer-Animated Film Is Made

Illustrated with actual artwork created by

Pixar Animation Studios

By JEFF KURTTI

DISNEY PRESS

New York

Adapted from
The Disney/Pixar Film
A Bug's Life
Produced by Darla Anderson and Kevin Reher
Directed by John Lasseter and Andrew Stanton

For Shawna, Jesse, and Darby
—J. K.

For more Disney Press Fun, visit www.DisneyBooks.com

Photo credits: Page 10: © Charles Melton/The Wildlife Collection; page 11: top © Michael Francis/The Wildlife Collection;
bottom right © Ken Deitcher; bottom left © Charles Melton/ The Wildlife Collection;
page 12: © Ken Deitcher; page 13: top © Tom Vezo; bottom: © Tim Laman;
pages 14–15: © Jonas Rivera; page 41: © Jonas Rivera

Contents

Concept sketch by Geefwee Boedoe

Foreword

I truly love the medium of computer animation. It has influenced the way I look at art. When I started out as an animator, I was drawing animation by hand. I was always excited by the way a simple artist's line could become a drawing. Now that I've been working with computer animation I have become fascinated by how painters and illustrators define light and space three-dimensionally.

Once I began working in computer animation, I started to wonder about which subjects would lend themselves best to this medium. When my colleagues and I were discussing ideas for our next feature film, a topic that immediately came to mind was insects. On one level it was because of the tremendous beauty with which they are formed and the artistic possibilities stemming from the environments where they live. We knew that effectively reproducing this world would be one of the greatest artistic challenges we had ever faced.

Another reason bugs came to mind was because we knew they had the potential to be the subjects of a really good story. No matter how beautiful the images in a film are or how impressive the technology used in creating a film, they will always be secondary to a good story.

When we start thinking about a story, there are two things we strive for: humor and heart. The humor needs to work on several levels. Not only do kids have to find it funny, but we want the parents with them to have a good time as well.

Then there's heart. As a huge fan of Disney films, I have always loved how for every laugh, there was a tear. And the characters are so sympathetic, so endearing, that an audience feels that they share in that character's joys and sorrows. That's heart. As filmmakers, we know that the key to achieving heart is to make a character as believable as possible. In the Behind-the-Scenes section of this book, you'll see that countless hours were devoted to all of the tiny details that make the world of *A Bug's Life* completely convincing.

I think the secret of our success lies in the hundreds of talented people who work on our films. My colleague Ed Catmull (one of the true pioneers of computer animation) said something to me early on in my career that probably influenced me more than anything else. I asked him once how he was able to get so many great people to work with him and he answered, "I always try to hire people that are smarter than myself!"

So I'm pretty lucky. I go to work each day with people who are smarter than me. Together, we work

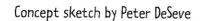

Concept sketch by Peter DeSeve

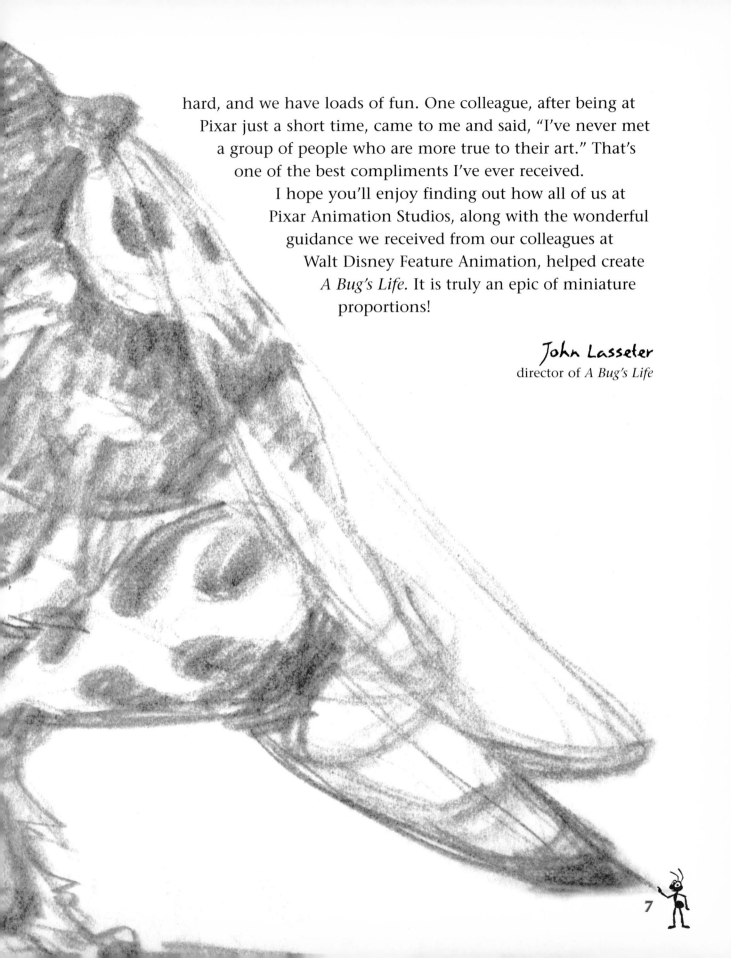

hard, and we have loads of fun. One colleague, after being at Pixar just a short time, came to me and said, "I've never met a group of people who are more true to their art." That's one of the best compliments I've ever received.

I hope you'll enjoy finding out how all of us at Pixar Animation Studios, along with the wonderful guidance we received from our colleagues at Walt Disney Feature Animation, helped create *A Bug's Life*. It is truly an epic of miniature proportions!

John Lasseter
director of *A Bug's Life*

7

Concept art by Geefwee Boedoe.

Inspirations

Although there are many differences between computer animation and traditional, hand-drawn animation, many of the steps in creating each are similar. The most important step in the process is story. *A Bug's Life* began with the film's codirectors, John Lasseter and Andrew Stanton, along with the head of the story department, Joe Ranft, looking at children's stories. "We were trying to come up with another idea—and this was even before *Toy Story* came out," Andrew Stanton recalls. "Joe Ranft and I were laughing about stories *not* to make in animation. So, joking like that, we ended up laughing about 'The Ant and the Grasshopper.' It was one of those moments where I stopped midlaugh and said, 'Wait. That's not funny. That's interesting.' We started talking about it, and looked up the Aesop fable."

Aesop's Fables is a collection of stories attributed to a Greek slave named Aesop. Each of the fables is a story with a moral at the end. "The Ant and the Grasshopper" tells the story of a carefree grasshopper who sings and plays all summer, while the industrious ant colony toils, storing their food for winter. When winter comes, the ill-prepared grasshopper comes to the anthill begging for food and shelter.

The grasshopper versus the ant, or in this case, Hopper vs. Flik. Rough storyboard by Joe Ranft.

"When the grasshopper's starving in the winter and comes asking for help, the ant says, 'You didn't work all summer . . . too bad,' and shuts the door in his face!" Stanton says. "That made us ask, 'Why doesn't the grasshopper just go get his buddies and come back and *take* the food?' This was the starting point for *A Bug's Life*."

"Story drives it all," John Lasseter says. Pixar's goal for its next film was to find a story that was best told in the medium of computer animation. The story must be chosen not to "show off" computer technology, but to *use* the medium to express an interesting, meaningful story.

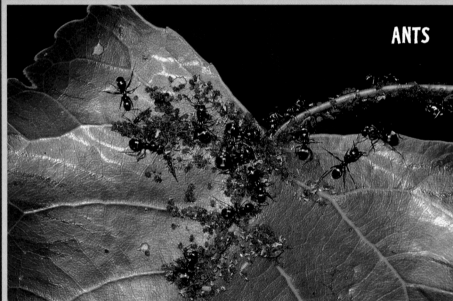

ANTS

Animators studied real insects to create characters that were both accurate and sympathetic.

10

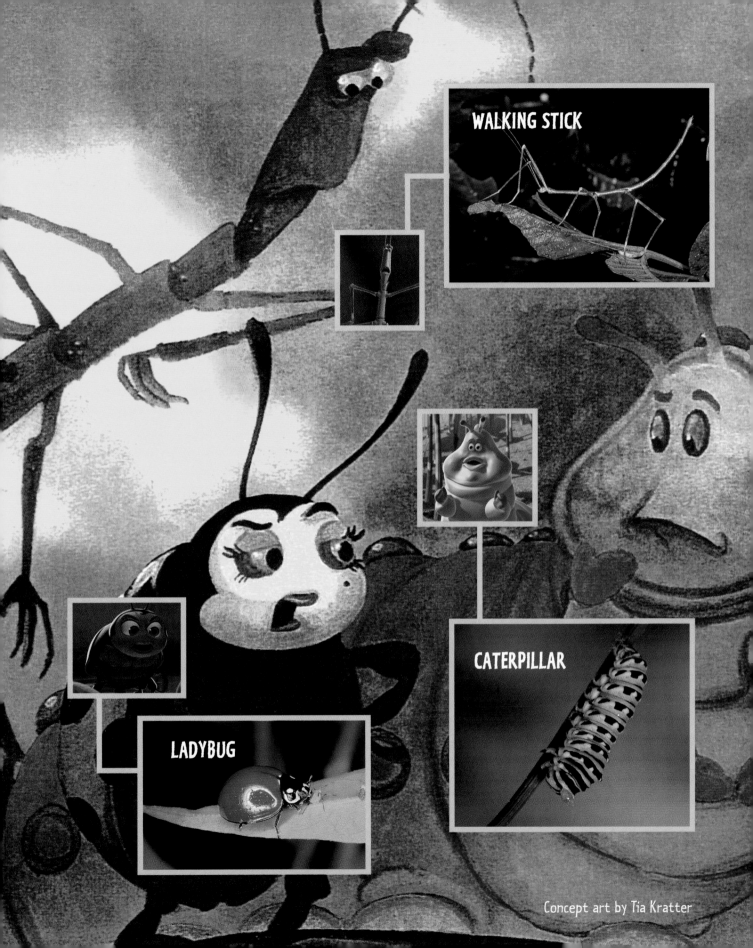

WALKING STICK

CATERPILLAR

LADYBUG

Concept art by Tia Kratter

"We have to think about what looks good with this medium," Joe Ranft says. "Plastic toys look good. Humans maybe *don't* look so good. Bugs seemed to be right."

"When you really study bugs, there's a tremendous *beauty* about them," John Lasseter adds, "and the way that they're made, the way they exist in nature. The exoskeletons, the color, the iridescence, the translucence: all these properties translate to our medium so beautifully."

Lasseter—who is still very much a kid at heart—also admits, "I've always loved bugs."

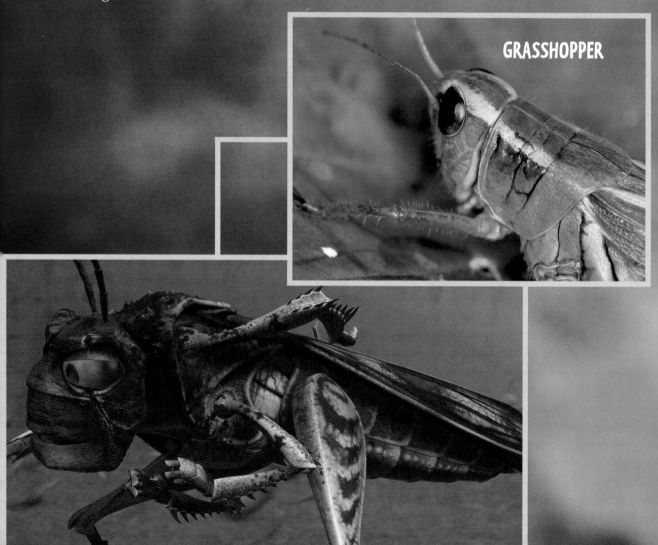

GRASSHOPPER

PRAYING MANTIS

RHINO BEETLE

One of the first things the makers of *A Bug's Life* did was to get down and get dirty. Production designer Bill Cone remembers, "Early on I went out looking around in nature, just crawling around on my belly with a camera. I shot a lot of photos. My biggest discovery was that the world is much messier and more complex than you ever imagined. But there are also all these great patterns in nature, in the leaves, and in the rocks. That became the nature of our world. That was our palette to play with."

Concept art by Bill Cone (top) and Robin Cooper (bottom) helped animators create a realistic world for the bugs.

Paul Kratter's concept art (below) shows life below the grass.

"We tried to take a video camera down low, but we were limited by the size of even the smallest ones," John Lasseter remembers. "A couple of the engineers got together and said, 'We can make a little camera.' (I love working at this company, 'cause it's full of geeks!) So they got a bunch of parts, and made this *tiny* video camera. We named it BugCam. It was mounted on a stick with little wheels, and we could put it way down underneath the base of plants, down in the grass where it looks like trees. We started looking at the world from a bug's point of view."

A Bug's Life
The Film Story

Ant Island bustled with activity.

"We're on schedule, right?" Princess Atta nervously asked Thorny, a member of the Royal Council.

The Queen approached, looking at the food heaped on the offering stone before them. "So, how's my daughter doing on her first official job?"

"Oh, Mother," Princess Atta sighed, "I just don't think I'm cut out for this."

"It's the same every year. They come, they eat, they leave," the Queen soothed. "You don't become a queen overnight, Atta."

Suddenly, a tall stalk of grain zipped through the air and fell squarely on the Princess. At the edge of the grainfield, Flik, a worker ant, had found a new way to collect grain. He had created his own mechanical harvester, which was strapped to his body. After each stalk was cut, and its grain shaken into a holding basket, the used stalk was ejected by a spring. Flik was so pleased with his automated marvel, that he didn't notice that his cast-off stalks were landing dangerously close to the Royal Family and Royal Council!

"Hey!" roared Thorny.

Atta knew Flik meant well, but his brand of individuality threatened the ways of the colony.

"Please, Flik, just get in line and pick grain like everyone else," Atta chided.

"I'm never gonna make a difference," Flik lamented, as he walked back to work with Princess Dot, Atta's younger sister.

"Me neither," Dot said. "Everyone says I'm too little."

"Being little's not such a bad thing," Flik assured the young princess. He picked up a small pebble. "Pretend that this is a seed. Everything that makes a gigantic tree is already contained inside a tiny little seed. All it needs is some time to grow."

Dot smiled up at Flik. Just then, the shriek of the alarm sliced through the air. All over the island the ants dropped their work and scurried toward the entrance of the anthill.

"Wait for me!" Flik shouted. As he ran past the offering stone, the spring from his harvester popped out, knocking one of the legs out from under the stone.

"No!" Flik yelled.

All of the food that had been collected slid off the stone, cascading over the edge of Ant Island and out of sight. In the distance, an ominous buzzing sound could be heard.

"Princess Atta," Flik panted as he reached the anthill, "there's something I need to tell you!"

Suddenly the buzzing stopped. Heavy footsteps stomped on the ground overhead. "Hey, what's going on! Where's the food?"

Atta glared at the Flik. "What did you do?" she demanded.

"It was an accident," Flik replied weakly.

Huge grasshoppers burst through the ceiling, sending the terrified ants scurrying in every direction. Flik looked up to see a particularly mean-looking grasshopper. He was the leader of the group.

"H-H-Hopper . . ." Flik stammered.

"So, where is it?" Hopper demanded. "WHERE'S MY FOOD?"

"Um, isn't it up there?" Atta asked meekly.

"Do I look *stupid* to you?" Hopper said angrily. "If it was up there, would I be down here looking for it? There are still a few months till the rains

come, and I'll come back then. But if you don't have our food ready like you're supposed to, I can't guarantee your safety . . ." the cruel grasshopper threatened.

The ants heard low growls from a darkened corner. Held on strong leashes by two grasshoppers was a snarling, drooling monster of a grasshopper—Thumper. Hopper snatched little Dot up from the floor and held the frightened princess out to the slobbering, snapping Thumper.

"We'll be back at the end of the season, when the last leaf falls. You ants have a nice summer," Hopper sneered. Then he abruptly dropped Dot and left with his gang.

The colony all turned to stare at Flik.

"Well, Flik," Atta prompted, "what do you have to say for yourself?"

"I was just trying to help," Flik replied.

"Then help us," Mr. Soil scoffed. "By *not* helping us."

"Help. . . help. . . helpers. . . that's it!" Flik had an idea. "We could find bigger bugs to come here and fight, and forever rid us of Hopper and his gang!"

"Who would do a crazy thing like that?" Dr. Flora asked.

"I volunteer!" Flik said.

An angry rhino beetle reared its head up and roared ferociously. A black widow spider stood in the shadow of the towering beetle, cracking a shoelace like a fearsome whip.

"Back, you horrible beast!" the spider shouted. "I have no fear of you!"

He reared back to roar again, when the spider accidentally hit him with the whip. The beetle broke into tears.

"Oh, I'm so sorry, Dim," the spider comforted the beetle. "Show Rosie the owie."

The audience booed.

"What a disappointment!" complained a fly as it zipped out of the tent past an aging banner that read: P. T. FLEA'S WORLD'S GREATEST CIRCUS.

P. T. Flea, the scruffy ringmaster and owner of the sorry circus, saw his audience disappearing. "You bozos get out there now!" he hollered to the clowns waiting behind the curtain.

"What's the point of going out there?" Slim the walking stick asked dramatically. "They'll only laugh at me."

"That's because you're a *clown*!" P. T. blustered.

Concept art by Bud Luckey

The clown act didn't fare any better than Rosie and Dim had. Francis, the ladybug, got into a fight with some rowdy flies, who thought that just because he was a pretty, colorful ladybug, that Francis was a girl. But he was a boy, and a pretty tough one, too.

Manny, the praying mantis, and Gypsy, his lovely wife, attempted their magic act, only to be booed off the stage. Seeing the last of his dwindling crowd leaving the tent, P. T. Flea jumped into the center ring.

"FLAMING DEATH!" he hollered at the top of his tiny lungs. All the departing flies and bugs stopped and returned to their seats. "Flaming

Death" sounded promising.

"I hold in my hand THE MATCH," he announced. "The match that decides whether two bugs live or die this evening. In a moment, I will light this trail of matches, leading to a standing sheet of sticky flypaper doused in lighter fluid!

"Aimed directly at the fly-paper are Tuck and Roll, the pill bug cannonballs! Their only hope of survival is our mistress of the high wire, Rosie, who must plummet down to these two posts and spin a web of safety in less than fifteen seconds!"

In the blink of an eye there was a giant flash of flame and a huge mistake. A charred P. T. stood in the middle of the smoke and ash, as the clowns, a few seconds too late, doused the humiliated ringmaster with water.

"You're fired!" P. T. screamed at the frightened circus bugs.

It was twilight when Flik finally arrived in The City. As he walked down the busy street, two bugs were thrown in his path, evicted from a seedy-looking saloon.

"And stay out!" came the shout from inside.

Flik was looking for tough bugs to defend Ant Island from the grasshoppers, and it looked like this place might be where he could find them. As Flik made his way toward the bar, he passed a table of very depressed-looking insects.

Just then, the two flies who had made fun of Francis at the circus entered the room. "Hello there, girlie bug," one of them jeered.

Francis kept his cool, but whispered to Slim, "Get ready to do the 'Sherwood Forest' bit."

Painting of the Bug Bar by Tia Kratter, layouts by Bob Pauley

Flik turned to see Francis grab Slim like a quarterstaff, as the caterpillar, Heimlich, joined him in a heroic leap toward the flies.

"Huzzah!" Francis yelled. "Stand back! We are the greatest warriors in all the shire!"

Flik's eyes widened in awe. "Warrior bugs . . ."

As the fight between the circus bugs and the rowdy flies broke out, the saloon (housed in a can) began to tip, rolling over and barreling down the street until it crashed into a post. The crash left the circus bugs on top of a mound of unconscious and bewildered flies, making the bugs look as heroic as they ever would.

Flik ran over to them. "I've been scouting all over for bugs with your kind of talent!"

"A talent scout!" Gypsy excitedly whispered to Manny.

"I'm from an ant colony just east of here," Flik explained, "and some grasshoppers are coming to our anthill at the end of the season."

"Grasshoppers, eh?" Francis said, imagining a whole new audience for their circus. "We can handle 'em!"

At the edge of Ant Island, Dot sat atop a clover and spotted the approaching bugs. "Flik!" she cried. "He did it! He did it!"

Dot ran up to Flik, who gave her an affectionate hug. "Flik! I knew you could do it!" the little princess said.

Cautiously, the ants all crept into view. The Queen was impressed with the crew of hired bugs. "Well, my boy," she congratulated Flik, "you came through."

Atta had her doubts, however, and quickly huddled the Council together in conference.

Slim, observing the royal huddle, whispered to Francis, "We're losing the job!"

Francis thought fast, and flew up to Dim's horn. "Your Majesty, ladies and gentlemen, boys and girls of all ages! When your grasshopper friends get here . . . we are gonna KNOCK THEM DEAD!"

The colony roared their approval.

That afternoon, a formal banquet was held in honor of the visitors. As the crowd broke into a wild ovation, Princess Atta rose to address the colony and express their gratitude to the visiting "warriors."

Rosie realized that this was a big mistake. "But we're not warriors, we're circus performers," she whispered to Flik.

Flik froze. Quickly, he gathered the bugs together where the other ants

couldn't hear them. *"Circus bugs!"* he screamed. "How can you be circus bugs?"

"You made us think you were a talent scout!" Manny protested. "Good day to you, sir. Gypsy, come."

"Wait! You can't go! You have to help me!" Flik cried. "Flik?" Atta called from behind the tall grass.

"Princess Atta! What a nice surprise," Flik stammered.

"Just what exactly is going on?" Atta asked.

Flik watched the circus bugs disappearing from view through the tall grass. He turned quickly back to Atta. "Could you excuse me, please?"

Flik begged them not to go, but when the bugs reached the edge of the island, they flew away. Flik jumped off the cliff after them, grabbing Slim, who was being carried by Francis.

"Okay, Flik," Slim said. "Let go."

Suddenly, Flik *did* let go, and began running! "*Run!*" he shouted.

The circus bugs turned to see a massive sparrow! And in the sky above them was Dot, hanging from a floating dandelion puff.

As the sparrow flew toward her, Dot screamed and let go of the dandelion puff. Francis quickly flew to her, and caught her just inches above the hard riverbed. Not being able to stop in time, they accidentally flew into the gorge. A loose rock fell after them, conked Francis on the head, and then pinned his leg.

"Yoo-hoo! Mr. Early Bird!" The sparrow looked up to see Heimlich, a caterpillar, balanced atop a wobbly Slim.

With the sparrow distracted, Dim and the rescue brigade flew to the gorge. Rosie spun a safety net and lowered it into the chasm along with Flik. Tuck and Roll clambered down the webbing and loaded Francis into the net, as Flik picked up Dot.

In the rescue net Francis came to, but as his wings snapped shut, he accidentally cut the line that had been holding the net closed. Clinging desperately to one another's antennae and the bits of Rosie's web that remained, Dim made for Ant Island.

He restored them to safety a breath ahead of the sparrow, zooming around Ant Island and into a prickly berry bush. The sparrow, not wanting to tangle with the thorny foliage, flapped about noisily and finally gave up.

Concept art by Bob Pauley (left and right)

The panting circus bugs lay inside the safety of the bush, catching their breath and recovering. One by one, they became aware of a loud and unfamiliar sound.

"What *is* that?" Rosie wondered aloud.

"That, my dear friends," Manny replied happily, "is applause."

Back at the anthill, Atta asked Flik, "How would you like to be the warrior bugs' assistant? You've got a great rapport with them, especially after that brave rescue. I mean, even Hopper's afraid of birds!"

"Say that again?" Flik was suddenly struck by another one of his great ideas.

"I said, even Hopper's afraid of birds."

Shortly after, Flik was huddled with the circus bugs, explaining his plan. "We are going to build a bird that we can operate from the inside."

Soon Manny was explaining Flik's plan to the Council, pretending it was the idea of the warrior bugs. "Then, when Hopper and his gang are below, we *launch* the bird and scare off the grasshoppers . . ."

Princess Atta was enthusiastic. She advised the colony, "If our ancestors were able to build this anthill, we can certainly rally together to build this bird!"

The colony cheered in support of the clever plan. Flik smiled proudly.

Far away from Ant Island, Hopper and his gang lounged in the sun at their tropical getaway. Two grasshoppers, Axle and Loco, were scheming about how they could get out of going back to Ant Island. They convinced Molt, Hopper's younger brother, to go to Hopper and suggest that a return to Ant Island was unnecessary.

Molt nervously approached Hopper with the suggestion. "You see, I've been thinking," Molt stuttered. "Why go back to Ant Island?"

Hopper looked at Molt in mounting fury.

"Those puny little ants outnumber us a hundred to one," he bellowed, "and if they ever figure that out, there goes our way of life! It's not about food, it's about keeping those ants in line! That's why we're going back!

"Let's ride," Hopper snarled, and the grasshoppers headed back toward Ant Island.

Once again, Ant Island bustled with activity. But this time, the ants were working for themselves, to protect their colony.

Leaves were cut, sticks milled, nutshells cracked to create their bird. With every hour that passed, their structure looked more and more like a real bird. Finally, it was ready. Together, the ant colony raised the bird up to its "nest" in the tree.

A huge accomplishment like that deserved a celebration. The circus bugs and all the ants threw a huge party. Cornelius and Rosie led a conga line that wound all around the island, Dr. Flora danced with Tuck and Roll, and even Princess Atta did a limbo dance.

Flik gathered the circus bugs, and let them know that he had arranged for them to be able to leave quietly. "Dim don't wanna go," the giant beetle said softly.

Flik's eyes brimmed with tears. Atta came up to them, gushing enthusiastically, "Look at this colony! I don't even recognize them! And I have you bugs to thank for it . . ."

The moment was interrupted by the sound of Thorny's alarm. The party stopped, and Atta cried out, "Battle stations, everyone!"

Instead of the pack of grasshoppers they were expecting, P. T. Flea's circus train stormed into the middle of the celebration. "Greetings! I am looking for a band of circus performers!" P. T. called out.

The circus bugs, seeing the trouble they were in, tried to skitter away, but P. T. spotted them. "You guys, Flaming Death is a huge hit! You have to come back!"

"You mean, you're not warriors?" Atta asked in disbelief.

With the discovery of the circus bugs' true identity, the Queen immediately lost faith in their plan to use the bird. "We're going to pretend this never happened," she commanded. "I suggest you all leave."

"But the bird!" Flik pleaded. "The bird will work!"

"You lied, Flik. To the Queen, to the colony . . . you lied to me," Atta said.

Flik looked around at the angry eyes of the entire colony, and then back at Atta. "I was just afraid that . . ." Flik hung his head. "That you'd think I was a loser."

"I want you to leave, Flik," Atta said softly. "And this time, don't come back."

Flik bowed his head and followed the humiliated circus bugs as they left the island.

At dawn, the sun rose on a weary line of ants hauling grain from the anthill to the offering stone. The drone of buzzing in the distance signaled the approach of the grasshoppers. One by one, the menacing villains emerged and surrounded the ants in front of the offering stone.

"You little termites!" Hopper screamed. "I give you a second chance and *this* is all the food I get?"

"But Hopper," Atta pleaded bravely, "it's all we can spare!"

Hopper led his gang into the anthill, where they quickly discovered a food chamber filled with grain.

"This wasn't part of the deal," Atta persisted. "You can't take it! We'll starve!"

Hopper roughly pushed Atta into the food pile. The Queen moved to help her daughter, but Hopper grabbed her arm. "No, no. You're staying with me, Your Highness," he menaced, leading the Queen outside. There he turned and shouted to the ants, "Not one ant sleeps until we get every scrap of food on this island!"

From a safe distance, Dot and her Blueberry Troop watched. "Quick, to the clubhouse!" Dot urged.

From inside the hideout, the ant girls overheard two of Hopper's thugs bragging to one another.

"Here's the plan," one said. "We're gonna work 'em till they drop. Then Hopper's gonna squish the Queen to remind 'em who's boss!"

Dot was horrified. "I'm gonna get help," she told the others. The little ant climbed out, carefully hiding behind a blade of grass. Then she turned in the opposite direction—only to run smack into Thumper!

He reached for Dot, cackling wildly, but she thought fast and dashed between his legs. Dot ran and flapped her little wings, but they were barely lifting her from the ground.

Thumper kept stepping menacingly toward Dot, forcing her backward toward the cliff. She plummeted over the edge. Satisfied with his work, the cruel grasshooper flew away.

Just then, Dot rose slowly . . . flying! She hovered for a moment, surprised at this latest development, then zipped off. She had to find Flik!

In the light of the setting sun, P. T.'s circus wagon trundled along. Inside the wagon, the circus bugs sat glumly. Flik was the most miserable of all.

"Flik! Wait!"

"Dot?" Flik said.

Princess Dot caught up with the wagon and lay panting on the floor. "You—you have to come back. Hopper's gonna squish my mom!"

Flik felt worse than ever. If he had just stopped getting those *ideas*, none of this would ever have happened.

"The bird!" Gypsy said.

"The bird won't work," Flik

muttered. "Let's face it. The bird is a guaranteed failure . . . just like me."

Dot buzzed outside and back again, carrying a pebble, which she handed to Flik. "Pretend it's a seed, okay?"

Flik picked up the pebble. Then he smiled and hugged Dot.

"Let's turn this wagon around!" Flik commanded.

Back on Ant Island, a sudden drumroll startled Hopper and the rest of the grasshoppers.

"Ladies and gentlebugs! Larvae of all stages! Rub your legs together for the world's greatest *bug circus*!" A bright spotlight pierced the shadows, and the circus wagon, with Slim at the reins, appeared.

Thinking quickly, Slim explained that the circus had been invited by Princess Atta to perform for some honored visitors. "I guess we could use a little entertainment," Hopper snarled.

As the circus performance continued, the distracted grasshoppers did not notice Flik and the Blueberries silently scaling the tree where the "bird" was "nested"—but Princess Atta did.

Manny selected the Queen as a volunteer for his disappearing cabinet trick. The Queen disappeared, and Gypsy floated out of the cabinet in her place. As Hopper was demanding the return of his hostage, he heard a piercing screech above him.

Hopper looked up to see a bird swooping right at him. Terrified, Hopper didn't know which way to run. He turned to see Slim running toward him.

"Oh! My eye!" Slim screamed, smushing a berry into his face to look like blood and collapsing at Hopper's feet. "Help me!"

The ants took Slim's lead and began faking the aftermath of a bird attack.

Concept art by Tia Kratter

Completely unaware of Flik's plan to scare the grasshoppers, P. T. looked at the horrific spectacle before him. He grabbed a match. "FLAMING DEATH!" he screamed, jumping on a can of lighter fluid.

"No, P. T.!" Slim shouted, but it was too late. P. T. set the match to a stream of lighter fluid, and a column of flame shot directly at the fake bird.

"Flaming Death!" storyboards by Nathan Stanton

The burning heap fell from the storm-darkening sky and crashed to the ground. Flik, Dot, and the Blueberries struggled, coughing, from the smoking wreckage, only to be confronted by a furious Hopper.

"Did you think you could get away with this?" he screamed, grabbing Dot. "You think you can fool *me*?" he hissed. The colony stood frozen with fear, watching.

"Put her down, Hopper," Flik demanded, stepping forward. "I'm the one you want. The bird was my idea."

Hopper threw Dot to the ground and cut Thumper's leash. The slobbering monster knocked Flik down.

Hopper turned to the crowd. "Let this be a lesson to all you ants. You are not meant to have *ideas*. You are mindless losers put on this earth to serve *us*!"

"You're wrong, Hopper."

Hopper spun on his heel to see Flik rising painfully to his feet.

"Every year these ants pick food for themselves *and* you," Flik declared. "So who is the weaker species? Ants don't serve grasshoppers. It's you that needs us."

An enraged scream erupted from Hopper. He raised his foot as if to crush Flik, but Atta flew in and threw herself between her hero and this villain. Hopper laughed at her.

"Uh, boss," Molt interrupted timidly. "I hate to interrupt, but . . ." Hopper spun angrily at Molt, only to see his worst fear come true. The entire colony had moved in, surrounding the grasshopper gang.

"Get back!" Hopper screamed. All the ants locked arms. Grabbing at Atta, Hopper snarled, "You tell them what to do!"

"All right," Atta calmly said. "Charge!"

The ants charge—
storyboard by
Joe Ranft

As the ants and the circus bugs followed Atta's orders, a dumbstruck Hopper was engulfed by a swarm of ants. As the frenzied riot continued, Hopper made a desperate approach toward the Queen, but was stopped by the silken lasso of an alert Rosie.

The ants were about to shoot the trapped and humiliated villain out of the circus cannon when rain began to fall in huge drops—each easily twice the size of the average ant.

The impact of the raindrops knocked Hopper out of the cannon and Flik off his feet. Hopper's blood boiled. He loaded himself into the cannon again. When Dim landed on the firing mechanism, Hopper flew directly at Flik. Grabbing the unfortunate ant, Hopper buzzed up into the tree.

As Hopper rose above the tree, laughing evilly, Atta suddenly sped past, grabbing Flik out of his clutches.

Even in this time of danger, Flik had yet another bright idea. "Go that way," he told Atta, pointing.

They buzzed away in that direction, Hopper right behind them. Just as Atta and Flik cleared the bank, a raindrop slammed them to the ground. Flik pulled Atta to her feet, and hid her behind a rock.

"No matter what happens, stay down," he warned.

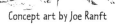

Hopper advanced toward Flik, scowling. "I can explain, Hopper!" Flik yelled. "Please! Please, don't."

Hopper closed in on Flik as he tried to back away. "I'll be back next season," he threatened. "But you won't!"

Suddenly, the screech of a bird broke through the sound of the storm.

"Well, what's this?" Hopper sneered, flinging Flik to the ground. Are there a bunch of little girls in this one, too? Hello, girls!"

But it wasn't a trick. The bird leaned down and snatched the startled Hopper off his feet, and offered the bewildered grasshopper to its hungry, chirping babies.

Concept art by Joe Ranft

Though the winter was hard, the colony and its new friends came through it just fine. Spring arrived and P. T. Flea was packing up his new and improved bug circus. Everyone was sad to see them go, even though they knew the circus would return to Ant Island when its tour was over.

P. T. turned to Flik. "Are you sure you can't come on tour with us?" he asked.

"Sorry," Flik replied. "My place is here."

Atta flew over to take Flik's hand. "Good answer." Then she turned to address the circus. "Thanks to you all, for giving us back our hope, our dignity, and our lives."

Then, the Queen stepped up to Atta and placed the crown on her head. "You've earned it, honey," she told her daughter. Atta then handed her tiara to her little sister, Dot.

The Queen was looking forward to early retirement and Atta would rule with Flik at her side. Never again would the ant colony fall prey to a gang of bullies like Hopper's. And they knew that they owed it all to Flik, an ant with ideas.

Behind the Scenes

Computers Don't Animate– People Do!

A lot of people are confused by the term *computer animation.* The computer has automated many of the functions that used to be executed by hand or by mechanical means, from reference books, to games, to the cash register at the supermarket. As a result, many people think that the characters of a film like *A Bug's Life* are simply programmed into a software system, and then made to move and act through some form of computer automation.

However, a better way to think about the process of computer animation is that the digital world has created a new set of tools for artists to use. "We are still binding brushes and stretching canvas, but for a different kind of medium," says Pixar's director of Studio Tools, Darwyn Peachey.

In fact, much of the creation of *A Bug's Life* didn't involve the computer at all, but came about in the way traditional animated films do. This traditional way of creating animated films is due in large part to the origins and people who work at Pixar Animation Studios.

Supervising animator Glenn McQueen works on Atta

Pixar, Disney, CAPS, and *Toy Story*

Pixar Animation Studios was founded in 1979 as the Computer Division of Lucasfilm, Ltd. At first, the group produced computer animation for movies like *Star Trek™ II: The Wrath of Khan* (1982), *Return of the Jedi* (1983), and *Young Sherlock Holmes* (1985). In 1985, they produced their first fully computer-

generated character animation, a short film called *The Adventures of Andre and Wally B.* From this short cartoon, the group realized that computer technology had great potential for character animation.

In 1986, the Computer Division of Lucasfilm, Ltd., became an independent company, and was renamed Pixar. (The name Pixar comes from a computer specifically designed to store large quantities of images and moving pictures, the Pixar Image Computer.) Between 1986 and 1989, Pixar made four more computer animated short subjects. Each of these shorts refined the techniques of computer animation, and the use of this technology in film storytelling. This series of shorts began with *Luxo, Jr.* (1986), followed by *Red's Dream*

(1987). *Tin Toy* (1988) was the first computer-animated short to win the Academy Award for Best Short Film (Animated). It was followed by *KnickKnack* (1989).

In 1986, Pixar and Walt Disney Feature Animation started a joint technical development called CAPS (Computer Animated

Scenes from previous Pixar films: *Knickknack* (top); *The Adventures of Andre and Wally B.* (middle); and *Tin Toy* (bottom)

Production System). The CAPS system allowed the inking and painting process to be done electronically. Instead of artists using brushes, they could now use an electronic color palette to create finished "paintings." Disney first experimented with CAPS for one scene in *The Little Mermaid* (1989), and has since gone on to use the system in all of its animated features.

At the same time, Walt Disney Feature Animation was looking for ways to increase the number of animated movies they released by experimenting with other forms of animation. The Pixar team, with a series of award-winning computer-animated shorts and several outstanding computer-animated television commercials behind them, felt ready to take the first steps toward the long-cherished goal of making a feature-length, computer-animated film. The two studios entered into another collaboration.

The result was *Toy Story,* a gigantically complicated application of the latest computer technology, used to tell the story of a group of children's toys whose world is the suburban bedroom of a little boy. *Toy Story* became the highest-grossing family film of 1995, earning more than 350 million dollars worldwide in its theatrical release, before becoming the top-selling video release of 1996. *Toy Story* also won a 1995 Special Achievement Academy Award.

Beyond all its technical achievements and creative ingenuity, *Toy Story* was a good *movie,* with sympathetic characters, a solid story, and a whole believable "world."

Woody, the lovable cowboy from *Toy Story*

Ready, Set, Story!

"In every story I do," director John Lasseter says, "I always strive to introduce the audience to a very familiar environment or situation but then show it to them in a way that they have never seen it before. Yet it makes sense—it's logical. Be it an insect, be it a toy, be it whatever. This believability goes into the whole look of the picture. It's something that underlines the design of the characters, the production design, the lighting design, everything."

Creating a World . . . One Leaf at a Time

As complex and technical as computer animation can sound, creating the world of *A Bug's Life* did not begin in the digital domain, but with the traditional visual development tools of drawing and painting.

"The first year was spent piling up big ideas, and then the settling of the big ideas, and seeing how they'd work out," art director/computer graphics painter Tia Kratter recalls. "We had these big stacks of photos, and all different kinds of exotic leaves and plants. I have piles of rocks, showing rocks of all different kinds of textures. My job was to define the color and texture of objects in the film. I was doing concept paintings that first year, just trying to do beautiful paintings and show how we could paint things in this film."

Concept art by Geefwee Boedoe (top); preproduction photos of trees, leaves, and textures helped animators create a world from a bug's point of view (bottom)

41

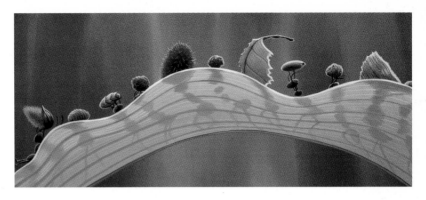

"One of the first things I realized was this interesting scale of things in the bug world," Bill Cone says. "When you're at that insect level in the dirt . . . qualities of scale start to appear. You can play with that. It becomes sort of a theme. We know we have big things—trees, rocks, grass, wheat. Well, now they're *really* big. A tree is Mount Everest. A rock is as big as a city block to these guys. That became a design approach—just thinking about these scale relationships."

"In *Toy Story* we got close to things, but never like *this*," Tia Kratter elaborates. "We had microscopes sitting around, where we'd start looking at leaves and the vein structure, or we'd start looking at textures on little bugs to see how we could get mileage out of that scale. Even a cookie box, and what happens when the edge of it frays, and how a bug might see that. I know how *I* see it, but how does a bug see the fraying edge of a box?"

One of the visual inspirations for *A Bug's Life* was a painting called "The Leaf Bridge Test." Tia Kratter created this painting based on a quick marker sketch by Bill Cone. Shadermeister (that's his real job title!) Rick Sayre explains, "It's a painting . . . that really got at the central visual feel of things. [It] brought together these vibrant colors and beautiful textures and combined them with sophisticated lighting and translucence. One of the things that John, and Bill Cone, and everyone wanted to see was this idea of translucence."

Concept art of The City by Glenn Kim (opposite page); the "leaf bridge test," concept art by Tia Kratter (top); production still (left)

43

"We saw," Lasseter explains, "that not only are parts of *insects* translucent, but basically, almost their entire *world* is translucent. Every grass blade is translucent with the sun shining through it. Every leaf that falls on the ground becomes a huge structure that you can go underneath and look up, and it's as though the entire thing's made of stained glass. Every flower. There are tremendous surfaces when you get down there, fuzzy and waxy and all different kinds of things."

"It's what helps give this movie the jewel–like quality it has," lighting director Sharon Calahan adds, "because translucency through a saturated surface like a leaf makes the color become very vibrant."

The beauty of leaves: concept art by Tia Kratter

Casting Characters

The artists could create the most believable settings in the world, but without equally well-developed characters and story, these settings would just be pretty pictures. John Lasseter says, "You make these characters very endearing to the audience. But the audience has to *believe* in those characters before they can feel emotion for them; that's a really important thing." Creating the characters and their personalities begins during the shaping of the film's story.

Flik

The film's "leading ant," Flik is an outgoing, earnest, well-meaning guy, but in contrast to everyone else in his colony, he's a nut. He'd like to march in line like everyone else, but these *ideas* keep coming to him, and he has to act on them. This is forever getting him into trouble.

The many faces of Flik: concept art by Bob Pauley (top left and bottom); production stills (top right and center)

Atta

Atta is the "Queen-in-training" of Ant Island. She is also inheriting a *huge* problem—the continuous cruelty of the villainous grasshopper gang. Atta has to learn to solve the problem—or learn to live with it. She is intrigued and amused by Flik, and genuinely likes him. Unfortunately, what she likes about him conflicts with her royal duties.

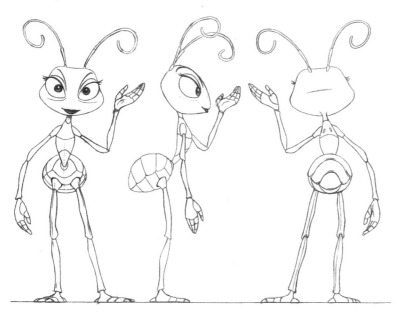

Concept art by Dan Lee shows Atta from three different angles (left); production still (top right)

Production still

Dot

She's just a little kid, but Dot is a can-do person. Though she's the smallest of the ants, she's very loyal, and she's got real spunk and courage. Dot is the only character who believes in Flik and supports him all the way.

Concept art of Dot by Bob Pauley

46

The Queen and Aphie

The Queen is wise, even though her manner is casual. She runs things, but with a sense of humor. Laughter is her way of coping. Aphie is an aphid, who is like the Queen's little lapdog. Like all lapdogs, Aphie is feisty, noisy, and protective of her master.

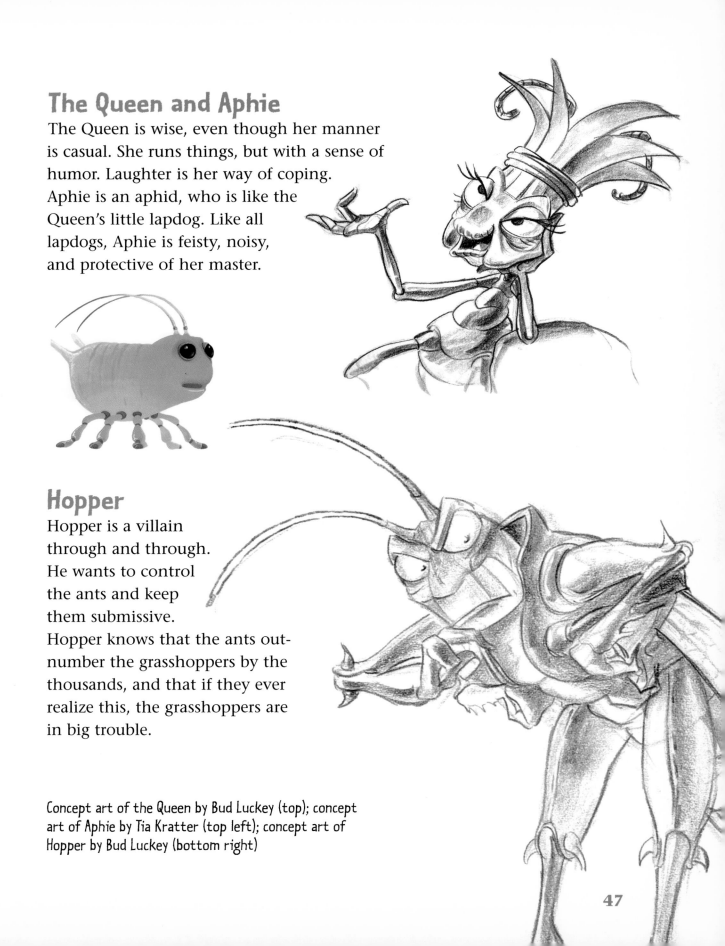

Hopper

Hopper is a villain through and through. He wants to control the ants and keep them submissive. Hopper knows that the ants outnumber the grasshoppers by the thousands, and that if they ever realize this, the grasshoppers are in big trouble.

Concept art of the Queen by Bud Luckey (top); concept art of Aphie by Tia Kratter (top left); concept art of Hopper by Bud Luckey (bottom right)

Molt

Molt is Hopper's brother, a dull-witted but funny follower, and a motormouth. Part of Molt's dopiness comes from the fact that he's really a nice guy at heart. That only irritates his mean big brother all the more.

The hapless Molt—concept art by Geefwee Boedoe

Concept art of Thumper by Peter DeSeve

Thumper

Thumper is another member of the grasshopper gang, but he's more like a mean attack dog. Thumper, with his senseless, brutal power, is always Hopper's last-resort threat.

P. T. Flea

The ringmaster and owner of the bug circus, P. T. Flea will do anything to make money. He's greedy, selfish, and cheap, but in a charming way. He fires the circus bugs because he's losing money and they've accidentally torched him. Once he sees that he can make money at it, though, he volunteers to be torched on a regular basis.

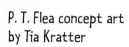

P. T. Flea concept art by Tia Kratter

Concept art by Rick Makki

48

Manny and Gypsy

Manny and Gypsy are the circus veterans. Together they form a magic act that has passed its heyday. Praying mantis Manny is a pompous, oblivious egotist, who would lose his head if it weren't for his long-suffering wife, the gypsy moth named Gypsy.

Concept art by Geefwee Boedoe (top left); concept art of Manny by Tia Kratter (top right); concept art by Bud Luckey (bottom left); concept art of Gypsy by Tia Kratter (bottom right)

Francis

Francis is a colorful ladybug, with large, limpid eyes, long eyelashes, and full lips. He also happens to be a *boy*, and one of the toughest boys around. The fact that he looks like a girl has given him a complex, turning him into a loud hothead with a large chip on his shoulder.

Concept art of Francis by Bob Pauley (top); concept art by Tia Kratter (left)

Heimlich

Heimlich is a jolly glutton in a rotund, spongy tube— a Bavarian caterpillar to whom life is a pleasure, mainly involving food. Heimlich can't wait for the day when he will transform into a beautiful butterfly.

Concept art of Heimlich by Bud Luckey

Slim

Slim is a stick bug who always feels miscast. He's a guy who is funny to others because of the way he looks—even though his idea of humor is much more highbrow. He is an intellectual who dreams of doing greater things. Because of his shape, though, he usually winds up as a prop.

Rosie

Rosie is a beautiful black widow spider who is the "conscience" of the circus bugs. She has a poised reaction to everything, and is both a moral compass and "den mother" to the group.

Dan Lee's concept art shows Slim's different attitudes (top)

Concept art of Rosie by Tia Kratter (left); concept art by Dan Lee (center); concept art by Jason Katz (right)

51

Dim

Dim is Rosie's performing partner. He is a big, dim-witted rhino beetle with good instincts and a simple, straightforward point of view.

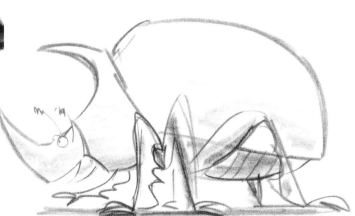

Concept art of Dim by Tia Kratter (top); concept art by Bob Pauley (right)

Tuck and Roll

Tuck and Roll are pill bugs who perform as acrobats. They don't speak or understand English. Tuck was hatched two seconds earlier than Roll—so he's a little more dominant. Tuck and Roll get into hotheaded, passionate arguments—which no one can understand.

Concept art by Bud Luckey (left);
Tuck and Roll concept art by Tia Kratter (right)

The Royal Council

As a group, the Royal Council represents the mentality of the whole colony. The members are resistant to change—and they're each a different flavor of pessimist. The council is composed of Thorny, Dr. Flora, Mr. Soil, and Cornelius.

Concept art of the royal council by Bob Pauley— from left to right is Thorny, Mr. Soil, Dr. Flora, and Cornelius

Thorny

Thorny is a tough little bug with a constant negative attitude—"Can't do it, it can't be done, I don't care how much time you've got, it just can't be done."

Dr. Flora

Dr. Flora is Ant Island's medical professional, and her form of pessimism is more matter-of-fact. She is resigned to the fact that things are bad, and that bad things happen. Dr. Flora can deal with the medical problems that arise, but she (and the rest of the council) ignore the *big* problems.

Mr. Soil

Mr. Soil is the teacher on Ant Island. He is an artist at heart, a performer, and is a little melodramatic.

Cornelius

Finally, there is Cornelius. He is just a curmudgeon. His attitude is, "We've *never* done it that way before—and I'm angry that you're even thinking of *trying* to change it."

Concept art by Max Brace

Talking Like Bugs: Character Voices

Characters aren't complete without character voices. Casting voices to the animated characters of *A Bug's Life* is just as important as casting the lead characters in a live-action movie. Voices must be carefully chosen to match the behavior, age, and even the shape of a character.

Voice performances are recorded before the animation is done, since the delivery and timing of the lines will influence the "acting" that the animator brings to the character. Often, a voice actor will also bring a further development to the character that hadn't been planned. A gesture, a different attitude, even the individual personality of the voice actor will influence the way the animator creates the performance of the character.

Over the production period of an animated film, a voice actor is often called in to record and rerecord up to half a dozen times. New scenes or revised dialogue from previous scenes are recorded. Usually, each individual voice actor is recorded alone. This leaves many of the critical issues of pacing and reaction to the directors, animators, and editors.

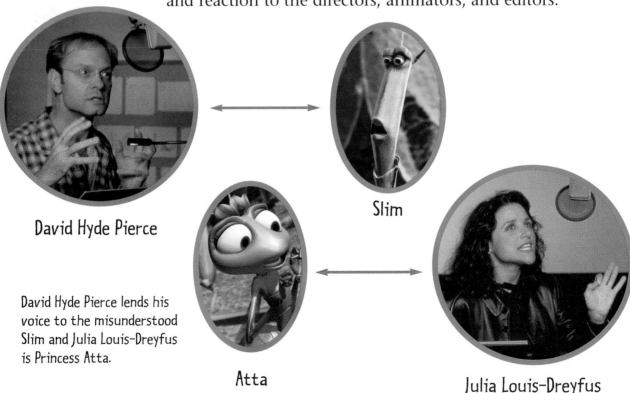

David Hyde Pierce

Slim

Atta

Julia Louis-Dreyfus

David Hyde Pierce lends his voice to the misunderstood Slim and Julia Louis-Dreyfus is Princess Atta.

54

Step-by-Step

Blueprint for A Bug's Life: Storyboarding

An animated film does not usually begin with a finished script, but as a "story breakdown" that is divided into sequences. The story team then takes these sequences and draws individual, shot-by-shot sketches. These story sketches are then pinned in sequence on large bulletin boards. When a storyboard is completed, the result looks and reads like a giant comic strip. The finished storyboards are a "blueprint" for the filmmakers. The boards show the basic layout, action, and dialogue for each scene. They also allow the story team to shift scenes, alter stage directions, or examine changes in their story without involving the time and resources of the rest of the production.

WHERE IS   MY

FOOD!

Storyboards by Max Brace

"Building" the Cast: Character Design

Once the story has been laid out, the *design* phase of characters development begins—character art director Bob Pauley and his art team can actually start "building" the physical and visual identities of the cast of "actors,"

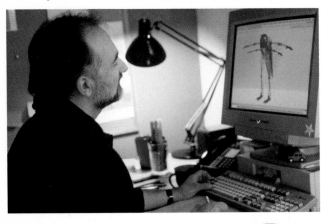

to support and expand on the attributes already defined by the story.

"One of the concerns early on was the 'ick factor,'" Pauley recalls. "We're taking on a cast of insects that are, by nature, very *disturbing* to a lot of people. So we have to filter out some of the 'ickier' elements, and make them more appealing overall. That's the direction we went: lose the

mandibles, stand them upright, accentuate those qualities that are appealing." However, the Pixar artists couldn't just *forget* that their actors are insects. "We wanted to create insects that weren't gross or ugly," animator Glen McQueen

Damir Frkovic, the technical director who designed the model for Hopper, inspects his creation (top). A model sheet by Dan Lee shows Atta's head (bottom).

MOUNTED AT A SLIGHT ANGLE OUTWARDS

BACK VIEW

BULBOUS TIP

56

ugly," animator Glen McQueen explains, "but we didn't want them to look like actors in bug costumes, either."

Once a basic design for a character is approved, a single concept artist finalizes the design. When a final design is approved, the artist then creates refined designs which are drawn onto model sheets. For each character, many model sheets will be created and refined, showing the character from all angles and in different poses. Physical sculptures are then created. These sculptures are known as *maquettes*. The drawings and sculptures are then given to a technical director, who builds a 3-D computer-generated model.

Every character in the film is created as a three-dimensional object *inside* the computer, like a digital "sculpture" or "doll" (kind of like a digital marionette without strings). The technical directors also define the range of movement possible for the character, and all the controls for the final computer model. Known as *articulated variables,* or *avars,* these controls are the "muscles" and "ligaments" of the character model.

—ANTENNAE STOCK
IS RIGID
ROTATE AND BEND
T JOINT

←—WHIP

←— STALK

Maquette of Flik by Norm DeCarlo (top left);
concept art of Flik by Tia Kratter (top right);
maquette of Atta by Norm DeCarlo (bottom left);
concept art of Atta by Tia Kratter (bottom right)

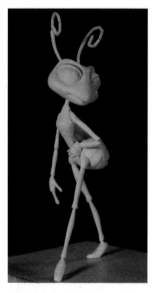

BASE
JOINT
(BEND +
ROTATE)

"The Central Nervous System": Editing and Story Reels

Meanwhile, as characters are developed, the story keeps chugging along. Storyboards that have been approved now move on to the story reel phase, which is the first step in editing the film. To build a story reel, the editors shoot the story sketches onto film in order, then edit them together in continuity with the working sound track.

In producing a live-action film, finished footage is edited after shooting is completed. For, *A Bug's Life,* the editors began the editing process of the story reel phase— and edited and refined each scene all through every stage of production.

As scenes are completed during the other phases of production, they are cut into the reel. This process results in a story reel that is continually revised and updated with scenes in various stages of completion, until all of the reels contain final, rendered animation. The result is a running "rough draft" of the entire film. "Our mission is to constantly keep the film in its most current state," editorial supervisor Bill Kinder explains. "All the other departments—from story through rendering in camera—stream through editorial.

"If the production is a body, we're the central nervous system," Kinder

continues. "Animation would be the heart or the soul, lighting would be the eyes, and layout is probably the right brain. The editorial department is the film at any given moment. We're the first on, and we're the last off."

Concept art of P. T. Flea by Bud Luckey (top); Second Assistant editor Torbin Bullock (left)

Computer-Animated Cameramen: Layout

From the story reels, scenes move into the layout phase of the production. The layout department blocks out all the characters' and objects' positions within the frame, as well as the frame composition and camera movement. If it were a live-action movie, layout supervisor Craig Good and his team would be the cinematographers of *A Bug's Life*.

"It's not like drawn animation, in which you have to paint a new background every time you want a different angle," explains Bill Reeves. "Our sets get built once, to fixed dimensions. As you position and move your camera, you see the changing view you'd have if you were walking through an actual physical space."

"We are working to create the visual composition of the film," Ewan Johnson, another layout supervisor explains. "Once [a scene] leaves the layout department it has ceased to be an idea and has moved into the realm of reality—if you can call what we do on a day-to-day basis reality. It's become a movie."

Concept art of P. T. Flea by Bud Luckey (top); Animator Doug Sweetland in action (bottom)

From Square to Rectangle: Wide Screen

One of the many differences between *A Bug's Life* and *Toy Story* is the shape of the movie screen. This shape is referred to as the *aspect ratio*, which is the ratio of screen height to screen width. *Toy Story* was created in a more "square" aspect ratio, one unit of height to 1.85 units of width, closer to the size of a standard TV screen. *A Bug's Life* has been created in a "wide screen" aspect ratio, one unit of height to 2.35 units of width, a rectangle-shaped screen. Usually, films made in wide screen are epic movies, like *Ben-Hur, 2001: A Space Odyssey,* or *Titanic.*

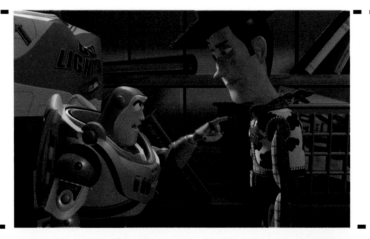

A Bug's Life aspect ratio (bottom) is much wider than the more square aspect ratio of *Toy Story* (top)—production stills.

Bill Cone and John Lasseter saw two advantages in wide screen. First, they could create numerous compositions of art and setting that would make *A Bug's Life* stand apart from other animated features. Second, the idea of making a wide-screen epic movie about the struggles of little tiny ants had a twist of irony.

Actors in Their Places: Character Animation

RULE #1
— HEAD HAS THE SAME FLEXIBILITY AS THE OTHER BODY SEGMENTS (FLEXIBLE BUT NOT FLOPPY)

WRONG LOOKS HINGED

RULE #2
KEEP THE FLOW OF THE POSE

Once the "cameramen" in layout have framed the camera positions and characters blocking for a shot, it is ready for another department—character animation. Unlike traditional cel animation, where the animator finalizes the character design and "makes it move" through individual drawings, the animation for *A Bug's Life* split this process into two steps: the building of the character model, and the animating of the character. As already discussed, every character in the film was created within the computer as a complete three-dimensional object. Then it was delivered to the animators. The animators make the characters move through the controls on the model—the "avars." Making the character move and act is still a painstaking, frame-by-frame process, but instead of *drawing* each action of the character, the computer animator uses the avars like marionette strings to control the movement of the character, from bending at the knee to twitching a lip.

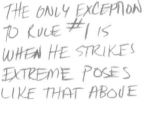

VERY RARE
✱ EXCEPTION

THE ONLY EXCEPTION TO RULE #1 IS WHEN HE STRIKES EXTREME POSES LIKE THAT ABOVE

A model sheet of Slim by Dan Lee shows how his upper body moves.

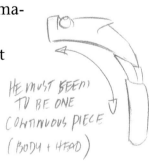

HE MUST SEEM TO BE ONE CONTINUOUS PIECE (BODY + HEAD)

Many animators on *A Bug's Life* had no computer training before working on this film. They came from traditional, hand-drawn animation, and stop-motion animation backgrounds. However, it is interesting to note that *acting* is of primary importance in computer animation. Drawing skill, of all things, is not—since a computer animator doesn't have to draw. He or she has to make a character move and *act* believably.

Dailies

Another difference between hand-drawn and computer animation is watching "dailies." In standard and hand-drawn animation, dailies are the *daily* shipment of film from the film lab where it is developed. The directors and animators can then review this film, and either approve it or make changes to it. During dailies in hand-drawn animation, for instance, the team might review a pencil-drawn test. Then, in order to change it, the animator has to go back to his drawing board and laboriously redraw the scene by hand.

At Pixar, dailies are a review of animation on video each morning, where the directors and animators can collaborate on revisions and alterations to the animation at stages of finish, from the most rough to the most refined. Changes and polish to the animation can be made fairly easily down to the tiniest detail, because the animator doesn't have to redo the character, drawing by drawing, frame by frame.

Concept art of P. T. Flea by Bud Luckey (left); the crew at Pixar reviews dailies (right)—director John Lasseter is fifth from the left in the third row back.

62

Shaders

Once the character animation is finalized, the shaders phase of the process begins. A shader is a piece of code in the rendering software that defines the surface appearance of an object or character. Every surface on every object and character in *A Bug's Life* has shaders applied to it, which determine the surface, its texture, and how it interacts with light. One specific type of shader is called a "texture map." Texture maps are used to add visual complexity to a surface.

"Shading is somewhere between lighting and scenic painting and finishing and manufacturing," Shadermeister Rick Sayre explains. "An analogy might be that shading and lighting are related in the way that modeling and animation are related. Modeling sets up the framework for these 'puppets' that are manipulated by the animators. Shading sets up a similar framework for the surfaces and the lights.

"There is no color or surface texture until shading gets started on it. What shading does is defines the surface appearance, as well as how surfaces interact with the lights. Shading tells the computer what the light source is, what the surface is, and how they work together. For example, you start with a plain desk. Shading will define whether that desk has legs made out of black powder-coated aluminum or anodized aluminum or metal or wood. Is the table varnished? What kind of wood is it made out of? What kind of surface treatment does it have? Has it had varnish put on top of it, or has it had just an oil stain?"

Shading reference for P. T. Flea by Tia Kratter (upper left); concept art of Rosie by Bob Pauley (center); Tia Kratter works on shading (bottom right)

63

Lighting

As in live-action films, each scene in *A Bug's Life* had to be lit. The lighting crew creates the mood and ambiance of a shot using every imag inable lighting source that a live-action filmmaking crew might use—and more. The lighting crew, however, did not have to contend with heavy equipment, power sources, or gels. Everything was controlled with a computer menu system.

The process of lighting in computer animation is a very collaborative design function, which occurs far earlier in the production schedule that it

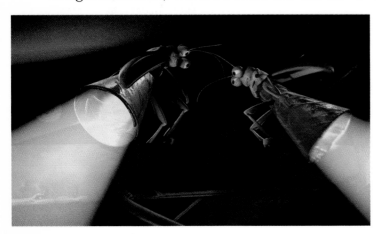

does on most live-action films. This forethought makes lighting more a part of the preliminary overall artistic *design* of the film, rather than a function that happens during the later production period.

Concept art by Bill Cone shows how lighting can be achieved through art (top). Production still (left)

Special Effects

In addition to the characters and their environments, every atmospheric effect in *A Bug's Life*—smoke, fire, and fog among them—had to be computer-generated. Meeting these challenges, which might be taken for granted in a live-action film, required a variety of techniques and systems.

Concept art of Tuck and Roll by Jason Katz

Motion Blur

An innovation created for *Toy Story*, "motion blur" is a technique for generating images that are blurred to show motion. Without this motion blur effect, characters and other moving objects would look static and unrealistic. *Persistence of vision* is the ability of a viewer to retain, or in some way remember, the impression of an image after it has been withdrawn from view. If an object moves too quickly for this perception, it will become a blur. (This is one reason that stop-motion animation often looks unreal. If there is no motion blur, the movement looks unnatural.)

Pixar's patented motion blur system is a process where pixels from a particular object are randomly distorted and displaced into a blur trail. The motion blur technique renders moving figures with an amount of "blur" proportional to their speed. Thus, their actions look natural.

Motion blur enables the insects in the film to fly realistically.

Fire, Steam, and Particle System

Subtle and complex effects like smoke, steam, fire, and sparks were created using a program called "particle systems." This technique renders these effects

as a pattern containing a large quantity of randomly moving shapes called "primitives." Smoke is actually a large number of tiny objects ("primitives"), moving together randomly, but in a fixed path.

The Flaming Death scene requires the use of special effects.

Finishing Touches

After all of these processes have been completed, *A Bug's Life* still has to go from inside the computer and onto film that can be projected at theaters. There are several steps in taking the computer information to finished film.

Rendering

Once all the elements of a shot are finalized (animation, shaders, lighting, effects, etc.), the shot moves on to the "rendering" stage of production, where all of the elements of the completed scene are rendered to their final state of polish. Each frame is rendered in its entirety as a final frame, since all of the data contained in a single *frame* of the film could take anywhere from forty-five minutes to two hours to complete! Rendering time was streamlined by rendering each *element* of a shot separately—background, foreground, and character elements.

These stills show how art looks before (left) and after (right)

Making A Bug's Life Sandwich: Compositing

Once all the elements are rendered, they are then "sandwiched" together to form the final frame. This process is called "compositing." Compositing is achieved with a tool called the Alpha Channel, another Pixar innovation. The Alpha Channel is a perfect "hold-out matte" for any given pixel on the screen. (A *matte* is used to "mask out" an area of the frame, so that another image, or images, can be combined in the same frame. A *pixel* is one of the thousands of tiny dots that make up a digital image.) With the Alpha Channel system, mattes that are perfect down to the pixel can be made for each of the elements that need to be composited together. The elements that have been rendered separately can then be seamlessly combined to form the final frame.

Turning Mood into Music: The Musical Score

A musical score is created for an animated feature to enhance the story being told in the film. The musical score, which usually runs almost the entire

Randy Newman creates the musical score for *A Bug's Life*.

length of the movie, emphasizes story points, adds drama, accentuates comedy, supports romance, and punctuates scenes.

The musical score was one of the final elements added to *A Bug's Life*. In collaboration with the directors, the score composer, Randy Newman, turned the emotion of the film into music. After Newman created his score, he conducted a full symphony orchestra while watching the film, scene by scene, so the music is in perfect sync with the on-screen action.

Bug Noises: Sound Design

In animated films, of course, there is no sound effect recorded "on the set." Every sound must be created to fit into the world that has already been visually created. Academy Award–winning sound designer Gary Rydstrom created the audio world of *A Bug's Life*.

Concept art of Hopper by Joe Ranft

Walt Disney Feature Animation executive vice president Tom Schumacher says, "What John Lasseter and Andrew Stanton do is perfect for Gary Rydstrom, because he's creating artificial sound to evoke real feeling, as opposed to creating *real* sound to create a real feeling. That is to say, the sound he'll make has no relationship to what an ant's foot would sound like when it falls, or what it would *really* sound like when an ant pushes a pebble or moves a grain of sand. Gary will have to *create* that sound, a fake sound that gives it a feeling of being real. That's his extraordinary gift."

The Theatrical Release

The final test of the animated filmmaker's work is the point when audiences actually get to see it. The final film prints, combining the fully rendered animation with the finished sound track, are released to theaters around the world. In the end, no matter how the film was made, in live action, traditional animation, or computer animation, audiences will be the final judges of whether it succeeds or fails.

"Audiences don't generally seek out a film based on the technology that was used in its creation," Walt Disney Feature Animation president Peter

Schneider says. "An audience seeks out connections to their hearts and minds—stories of interest, characters that captivate, all wrapped in an entertaining package."

"If we'd known how hard *A Bug's Life* was going to be when we started it, we might have run in the other direction," Pixar chairman and chief executive officer Steve Jobs admits. "We didn't want to rest on our laurels, so we bit off a lot . . . but we pulled it off. It's remarkable! My jaw just drops when I see, not just how it *looks*, but how the creative team has used their palette of technology to tell a great story."

Concept art of Heimlich by Joe Ranft

Glossary of Terms

Animator—An artist/actor. In traditional animation, the animator draws the character he or she is bringing to life. In computer animation, the animator moves the characters on the computer, with controls on the model called "avars."

Art Director—An artist who is responsible for the overall visual look or design style for either a specific area of a movie (character design, color styling) or the overall film (also see Production Designer).

Aspect ratio—The ratio of screen height to screen width. Most movies have a 1 to 1.85 aspect ratio. The "Academy Standard" ratio, and that of the standard TV screen, is 1 to 1.33 (also see Wide Screen).

Avars—(articulated variables) Points which operate like the muscles and tendons of the computer-animated character. The animator uses the avars like marionette strings, to control every movement of the character.

BugCam—A special miniature video camera created by Pixar engineers, which allowed the videotaping of environments from an insect's point of view.

CAPS—(Computer Assisted Production System) Computerized system that enables the traditional hand-drawn inking and painting process to be accomplished electronically. Instead of using brushes, artists now use an electronic color palette to create finished "paintings." The system is then used to composite the background, animation, and other art onto the final film.

Composer—A musician who writes the music for a film. Randy Newman was the composer of the musical score for *A Bug's Life.*

Compositing—The act of assembling the various levels of the computer-generated frame (background, foreground, character) into a single frame of film at high resolution in preparation for printing onto motion picture film.

Dailies—In standard and hand-drawn animation, "dailies" are the daily shipment of film from the film lab. The directors and animators can then review this film, and either approve it or make changes to it. At Pixar, dailies are a review of animated scenes on video each morning, where the directors and animators can collaborate in revisions and alterations to the animation at various stages of finish.

Director—The creative leader of a film project. He or she supervises actors, artists, writers, and other creative staff in a synchronized vision. On *A Bug's Life,* John Lasseter and Andrew Stanton were codirectors.

Editorial—Department responsible for the continual assembly of all film and sound elements on a project. Editing begins in story development and continues throughout production.

Concept art of Francis by Bud Luckey (top); concept art of Hopper by Peter DeSeve (bottom)

69

Effects (or special effects, or effects animation)—Those things in an animated film that move, but are not character animation, including smoke, sparks, rain, fire, or steam.

Field—Refers to a camera's vision—what the camera sees.

Frames—The individual pictures that make up a motion picture film. When viewed in rapid succession, frames create the illusion of movement. The standard number of frames per projected second of 35mm film is 24.

Layout—The department and process that blocks out all the characters' and objects' positions within the frame, as well as the frame composition and camera movement. At Pixar, the layout department is like the cinematography team on a live-action movie.

Lighting—The process that creates the mood and ambiance of a shot using every computer evocation of lighting source that a live-action filmmaking crew might use—and more. Lighting is considered more of an artistic or design element on most animated features, where as in most live-action films, lighting is simply illumination of the set.

Live action—Motion picture photography of real people and things.

Maquette—A three-dimensional physical sculpture of a character.

Matte—A "mask" that allows for the exposure or filming only of the area not masked. This, in turn, allows several separately created elements to be combined in the same frame.

Model—A three-dimensional object created within the computer, like a digital marionette without strings.

Motion blur—A technique for generating images that are blurred in the direction of motion. Pixels from a specific object are randomly distorted and displaced into a "blur trail." The motion–blur technique renders moving figures with an amount of "blur" appropriate to their speed, making their actions look real and natural. Pixar developed this technique so the car chase at the end of *Toy Story* would look real.

Particle Systems—This technique renders subtle and complex effects like smoke, steam, fire, and sparks as a pattern containing a large number of shapes, called "primitives," moving together randomly, but in a fixed path. The scene in *Toy Story* where Woody dunks his burning head into a cereal bowl is a good example.

Persistence of Vision—The ability of a viewer to retain, or in some way remember, the impression of an image after it has been withdrawn from view.

Pixar—The name of Pixar Animation Studios comes from a computer specifically designed to store large quantities of images and moving pictures, the Pixar Image Computer.

Pixel—Short for Picture Element, a pixel is a single point in a graphic image. Graphics monitors display pictures by dividing the display screen into thousands (or millions) of pixels, arranged in rows and columns. On color monitors, each pixel is actually composed of three dots—a red, a blue, and a

Concept art of Thumper by Bud Pauley (top left); concept art of Heimlich by Joe Ranft (bottom right)

green one—all converging at the same point. The pixels are so close together that they appear connected.

Producer—The person (often two or more people) who supervises the making of a film. On *A Bug's Life*, Darla Anderson and Kevin Reher were the producers.

Production Designer—The artist who creates and supervises the overall look of a film. The production designer oversees art directors charged with designing specific aspects of visual design (characters, color). Bill Cone was the production designer for *A Bug's Life*.

Rendering—The stage of production where all of the elements of the completed scene are generated from the computer in their final polish state and onto motion picture film.

Scale—The relative size or proportion of characters or objects to one another, or to the point of view of the observer. One of the ideas that made *Toy Story* and *A Bug's Life* interesting was showing the world we know in a different scale.

Scene—In animation, an individual cut within a sequence. In live action, a scene is called a shot or a cut, a sequence is called a scene.

Sequence—A portion of a film's overall story, usually centered on a location or a specific part of the story.

Shaders—A piece of code in the rendering software that defines the surface appearance of an object or character.

Concept art of Francis by Bob Pauley (upper left); concept art of Tuck and Roll by Bud Luckey (bottom right)

Sound design—The creation of an assortment of sound effects that make the audio illusion of reality correspond with the visual illusion of reality created by animation. Gary Rydstrom designed the sound for both *Toy Story* and *A Bug's Life*.

Sound track—The recording of dialogue, sound effects, and music that accompanies a motion picture.

Storyboard—A sequence of rough sketches, pinned together in consecutive order on a large bulletin board, which gives the film's creators a sense of how a story progresses.

Story Reel (or work reel)—A series of story sketches which have been shot on film, then edited together in continuity with the working sound track.

Story Sketches—The individual drawings that, when pinned together in sequence, make up a storyboard.

Translucence—Having the quality of permitting light to pass through an object, like a leaf.

Tools (studio tools)—The department that creates computer software tools for use by the various departments making a computer-animated film.

Wide Screen—Any film projection or video screen ratio larger than 1 to 1.33. The ratio of 1 to 2.35 is generally called "wide screen."

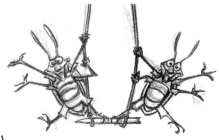

Bibliography

Buena Vista Home Video. *Toy Story Deluxe Laser Disc Edition and Supplement Material.* Burbank, CA: Walt Disney Home Video, 1996.

Buena Vista Home Video. *The Hunchback of Notre Dame Deluxe Laser Disc Edition and Supplement Material.* Burbank, CA: Walt Disney Home Video, 1997.

Hahn, Don. *Disney Magic: A Behind-the-Scenes Look at How an Animated Film Is Made.* New York: Disney Press, 1996

Lasseter, John, and Steve Daley. *Toy Story: The Art and Making of the Animated Film.* New York: Hyperion, 1995.

Maltin, Leonard. *Of Mice and Magic: A History of American Animated Cartoons.* New York: McGraw-Hill, 1980.

Schroeder, Russell. *Disney's Mulan: Special Collector's Edition.* New York: Disney Press, 1998. Thomas, Bob. *Disney's Art of Animation: From Mickey Mouse to Hercules.* New York: Hyperion, 1997.

Thomas, Frank, and Ollie Johnston. *The Illusion of Life: Disney Animation.* New York: Hyperion, 1995

Concept art of Atta and Flik by Max Brace

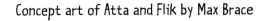